How to Become a Movie Extra

Tom Willett

ISBN: 10:1544827628
ISBN: 13: 978-1544827629

DEDICATION

Dedicated to you, Rocco, wherever you are.

CONTENTS

ACKNOWLEDGMENTS

There are two groups of people who helped me succeed in Hollywood Those who encouraged me to follow my dreams and those who told me I would never make it. I thank each of the people who offered me advice along the way.

First, my mom. She always had positive things to say about my chances of becoming an entertainer.

Second, Al Jarvis, who took a chance with me when I was 18. He let me do a stand up routine on his popular Los Angeles TV show, Make Believe Ballroom, in 1957.

Third, Bill Hess, who laughed at my jokes and gave me my first opportunity to succeed in radio.

Fourth, Joe Behar, who helped me become a movie extra in Las Vegas in 1979.

And finally, all the many people who told me it was impossible to make it in Hollywood. Your voices helped me to shift into high gear.

CHAPTER 1:
WHAT IS A MOVIE EXTRA?

A movie extra is the person you see in a feature film or TV show or commercial who is usually in the background of a scene, helping to establish the atmosphere for the shot. If the principles are in a restaurant doing their dialog, you often see other restaurant patrons in the background, or sometimes foreground, eating their meals and appearing to be chatting with their companions. They might be walking down the street behind the star of the movie, seeming to be going somewhere and not noticing the famous person they just passed. They might be part of the audience listening to someone speaking at a political convention or watching a sporting event or watching gladiators in combat in an arena, if that is part of the movie plot.

Extras do much more than just appear in the movie. Some extras will become photo doubles or stand ins. Some will do walla and others will be chosen to work as hand insert extras. If an extra happens to be a great dancer, he or she might be doing the dance number while they are dressed to look like the star. A few close up shots of the actor's faces as they speak their lines and then a distant shot of their great dance moves. A photo double does not have to look exactly like the lead actor to be used for an over the shoulder from behind dialog or action scene.

Walla is what background performers sometimes do in post production of a scene. If a crowd murmur has to be added to make the scene more realistic, the extras will provide "Walla, walla, walla " or some mumbling sounds to existing movie clips. Hand insert extras are filmed signing a document or shaking hands close up to emphasize a scene. Have some pictures that show your hands if you want insert work.

Your first day as a movie extra might find you in a crowd scene with a few dozen or few hundred other extras. You will be given a voucher by an Assistant Director. You will be told where to wait until you are placed in front of the camera. You might be within an arm's length of the camera or a football field away. You will be given a cue when to do your background action. You will hear someone say, "And... we are rolling..." Then another voice will say "Speed." Finally your cue, "Background." You do whatever you were directed to do. You walk or you dance or you pretend to eat or you applaud or you lean against a building. Then the word "Action" is for the principles who are doing dialog or action. The scene continues until it is finished and you hear the word "Cut." About five times out of six that is followed by "Back to one." You go back to your starting point and get ready for take two or whatever take is next.

The most takes I have ever done for one scene was slightly over forty. That was in the movie Pennies From Heaven with Steve Martin. In that movie I was a customer in the diner during the title song and dance sequence. I did have a close up shot where my face was closer to the camera than the principle's face. Vernel Bagneris danced past the diner in the title song sequence. I was seated in that diner.

Charlie Chaplain was known for sometimes doing hundreds of takes of a scene as he looked for nuances in expressions of the actors. Most directors move much more quickly than that.

When you do a scene you must remember where you were and what you were doing with each line of dialog. The reason for that is your first scene is probably the establishing shot. After that you repeat your background action for the coverage. That means they will move the camera to do a close up of the same scene with actor number one, then they redo the scene again to get actor number two and so on. There might be a need to do it all again for a drone shot that will be used as someone's point of view. Long days are common in making movies.

The common rule in Hollywood is each page of script is about one minute on screen. This varies greatly, of course. A thirty minute sitcom will have about thirty pages of script. Most feature films are about seventy to one hundred pages. On the first day of shooting, a script could be one hundred twenty pages, but during the production pages might be changed or added or deleted. The final script could be one hundred ten pages or one hundred thirty pages. That means your scene could be cut or changed.

I have worked in several movies where I was never used on camera. I have been in several movies and TV shows where my scene was filmed and not used. I worked at least two films where I was called back a month or two later to redo my scenes. They had changed the lead actor and they needed to do the entire scene again with the new actors and the same background performers.

A stand in is an extra who stands in for a particular actor or sometimes more than one actor during the movie or TV or commercial production. Some actors have their stand in chosen in advance. Most actors are given stand ins for the show by the production company. A stand in is considered a part of the crew. The stand in works every day the actor works.

You might get a call from casting with instructions to audition or interview for a stand in job in a movie. They will tell you which actor, often a big celebrity. The casting person will confirm your height and weight and current "look." Have you grown a beard since your last photo or added any weight or lost a few pounds? You must have a very good reputation as a person who is helpful to the movie or TV project.

At the audition you will be asked some questions. The producers want to know about you and how you respond is actually important. Finding the fine line between knowing your way around a set and being a ham is what will matter now. Everyone on the interview is the right height and weight. The production team wants to know how it will be working long hours with you. You can do it. Just be your nice self.

On the set the stand in is used for setting the lights for a scene and for getting the correct focus and technical adjustments. The stand in tells his or her actor any changes made after the rehearsal. The stand in works while the actor is going through wardrobe and makeup. If a mark on the floor is changed, the stand in tells the actor.

I have stood in for Harvey Korman, Pat McCormick, John Lithgow, Mel Ferrer, Christopher Lee and Robert Urich among many others.

A photo double might be used in an over the shoulder scene where one actor is speaking to the stand in who is dressed in the actor's wardrobe. The photo double might be in a scene where we see the actor from the chest down but we do not see his face, The photo double might be riding a horse or dancing or doing some karate moves. Photo double work does pay more than the standard rate for an extra. The dance rate is very high.

If you see someone's hand or hands in a movie, up close, that is most likely a hand insert that was filmed weeks after the establishing shot. Have some photos that show your hands on file with your extra agent. Hand insert shots include signing documents, playing piano or guitar, handshakes and reaching into a vault or cooking scenes.

Walla is just crowd sounds, not scripted dialog, that is added to enhance some scenes. Let your agent know if you want to do walla background sounds as well as on camera performances. Walla is done in a small theater type room where the action is on the screen and you are making the necessary sounds into a microphone.

CHAPTER 2: WHERE SHOULD I BEGIN?

If you happen to live in the Hollywood area you are all set to get started. Search online for "Movie Extra Casting Agencies." Call all the companies and ask when they are seeing new extra talent. Each agency will have a schedule, maybe one day each week for men and one for women. Most agencies will charge a fee of about $25 to take your picture and put it in their file. When you have registered, they will give you a phone number to call for work. That line will usually be busy. You will learn to dial while you are cooking or paying bills.

You eventually will work. If you are non union (SAG/AFTRA) in the US, you will try to become union qualified by getting three union vouchers from the Assistant Directors on the sets where some union member did not show up for work. That, plus the $3000 initiation fee will get you into SAG/AFTRA. Very expensive, but if you plan a movie career, it is worth it.

If you live in some other major US city, such as Nashville or Las Vegas, etc., search "Nashville movie extra casting" or "Las Vegas movie extra casting," etc. If you live in a remote area you might get a job working as an extra if you see a production company shooting somewhere. Walk onto the set and tell the security person you want to see the Second A. D. Tell the Second Assistant Director you are free for the next few days and would like to work as an extra. Maybe it will work and maybe not. Your best chance for working as an extra is to live in a major city. Hollywood is best.

You can get extra work in other countries, but you will most likely not stay busy enough to earn a living as an extra. Perhaps India would have enough productions to support background actors in the major cities, but I know only about the US.

Invest in pictures, resume and business cards that have your contact info and a small picture of your face. Your resume does not have to be filled with starring roles in major films. A head shot glossy picture with a resume stapled to the back is given to casting agents. A business card is given to Assistant Directors and anyone who might have helpful information. Even knowing other extras will be helpful.

CHAPTER 3:
REQUIREMENTS

You will need some pictures of yourself in various kinds of wardrobe. You will also need lots of wardrobe. You might start with one suit as I did, but add to your collection of clothing a little each month. The attire that will get you work is often available at thrift stores and on line at discount suppliers and costume shops. Do not have pictures of yourself in clothing with copyright logos. No team names or beverage brand names or funny sayings.

Men will eventually need a tuxedo, suits from different eras, such as the 1940s and 1950s, etc. Cowboy or Western wear with boots and hats, security guard uniform or police uniform and priest's collar all will add to your value to the production companies. Sweaters, including turtle necks and cardigans could come in handy for ski lodge scenes.

Women will need formal gowns and beautiful shoes for some scenes and a business suit for office and courtroom scenes. Slowly build an incredible wardrobe and get pictures of yourself in various dresses and coats and hats and uniforms. Check the attic for any 1940s dresses or shoes. A few hats and purses will help.

If you remember nothing else from this book, remember this; They don't need YOU for this movie or TV show. They do need your wardrobe. They do need your car. They do need your special skills and abilities. They need your stance when you walk across a room.

When I retired from being an actor and an extra, I had more than 35 suits. I had a couple of dozen pairs of shoes. I could be a 1950s character or I could look like today..My closet was crammed with clothes, but I knew people who had more wardrobe than I had. I did not have white tie and tails. I did not have a clown costume.

I had a priest's collar and shirt. That got me lots of work. I also had a nice police uniform which earned me many times what I paid for it. I received an extra $15 each time I wore a special outfit in a movie or TV show. I worked many shows as Abe Lincoln. The beard cost me $15. It paid for itself the first time I used it. Each time I purchased something unusual in wardrobe, I took a picture of myself wearing it and then I visited casting. I gave them the picture. If they did not want the picture it had already done its job. The next time they needed a cop or Abe Lincoln or a priest, they thought of me first. Casting knew me. I was never a pest. I visited only when I had something new to show them.

In movies and TV scenes I have been a cop, a prisoner, a priest, a president, a hunter, a hospital patient in robe and pajamas, a hit man in a 1930s trench coat, a cowboy and a musician with guitar and a musician with my own keyboard. All of that from my own wardrobe and personal props.

You will need a good car to get to and from the studios and location. The fastest way to get into movies on a somewhat regular basis is to be in the Hollywood area, registered with one of the extra casting agencies or all of those agencies and have access to, or own a vintage automobile. If you have a 1940s car and the production takes place in the 1940s, they will want you to drive your car in the scenes. You will receive the movie extra base pay plus a car check, which, for special cars, like vintage or a Rolls or a limo or a motor home or something unique, starts at $100 as a rule. For a regular car it is about one fourth that amount. Your car can get you to the set and it can get you into the movie. The same is true of motorcycles, trucks and even bicycles. A 1940s Jeep painted olive drab could get you work.

Your skills and abilities can get you into some good scenes and even get you converted to principle status which would make you eligible for a SAG/AFTRA membership, which, of course would require an initiation fee. The fee can be paid in installments. The daily rate of pay for a principle part is high. Check SAG/AFTRA for union rates and information.

Special skills and abilities would include, dancing very well, playing sports very well, karate and martial arts and courtroom artists. Also close order military drill and a familiarity with swords or weapons could be your ticket. Casino card dealers and precision drivers are always in demand.

If you look like a famous person, get a picture to the extra casting agencies of yourself looking like that person. Also get an acting agent to try to get you cast as that person, if you look like a president or world leader or Rock star or fictional character. You might also contact the A.D. of any show the celebrity you resemble might be working. They might need a photo double.

Some movies and TV shows pay extra for a dog or cat in some scenes. I have known many extras who walked their dogs in movie scenes. I did work with dogs, horses, a falcon, a leopard, a bear and an elephant.

CHAPTER 4: IS IT WORTH IT?

Is the pay received by an extra worth the effort? That will, of course, depend on you. Non union extra work might pay little or nothing. A union extra who works as a regular stand in on a show can make a very good living and earn some great retirement credits. An extra who works with some regularity in commercials will also make a very good living and have the benefits of a very good union retirement and pension pay. You could do extra work occasionally and have some "extra" income.

I worked about eight years as a Screen Extras Guild member. Then the Screen Extras Guild ceased to exist and Screen Actors Guild took over the jurisdiction. I lost the potential SEG pension. Then in 1988 I became a regular cast member of the TV series Dear John on NBC TV. I started earning SAG (Screen Actors Guild) benefits, including retirement credits. I now am retired and I have medical coverage. For me, the answer was, "Yes. It was all worth it." If I had not worked as an extra I would never have earned a pension.

The pay for a union extra in the US for 2017 is about $162 per day and about $189 per day for stand ins. There is a lot of overtime pay in movies and occasional overtime in TV shows. If you work in a union commercial you will be making about $400 per day. There are many ways to make more in any movie or TV or commercial production. Overtime pay, pay for working in smoke, travel expenses, pay for providing your own costume or uniform and Saturday and Sunday premiums.

Eventually, if you work on a lot of shows, you will be in the right place at the right time and you will be offered an opportunity to be upgraded. You might be a waiter or waitress in a scene and the director will decide the scene will work better if you say, "May I take your order?"

That simple sentence, one line, can result in many hundreds or even thousands of dollars in years to come. You will be paid the actor's daily rate which will be about $1000 or perhaps even a weekly rate if the scene continues to be shot for several days as you bring the food to the table and thank the customers. When the movie shows on TV you will receive a residual check in the mail. "Mailbox money" can be greater than the original payday, because the residuals come in year after year, getting smaller and smaller but there they are. I have received residual checks of less than one dollar on many occasions. Some of my friends have shown me residual checks of one penny. That was after taxes were deducted. Residual checks are sometimes the bulk of a busy actor's income.

The best pay for an actor or an extra is in commercials. The pay scale per day is over $350 for background performers and about $800 to $1200 for actors depending on many different classes of SAG/AFTRA commercials. If the commercial is shown often the principle will receive many, many residual checks. The background actor will be paid just for the day he or she worked. There are no residuals for background work. Some background performers will make very good pay just for background work.

When I worked as a background actor in a Hewlett Packard commercial, I received an allowance for holding and appearing to strum my own guitar, which they asked me to bring. I also received a lot of money that day for what is known as meal penalties. If the actor or background extra is not provided with a hot meal within six hours of the call time the production company must pay for the inconvenience. On the Hewlett Packard commercial we received eight meal penalties. In those days it was $25 for the first meal penalty and $50 for each one after that. It is worth it for the production company because they want to keep filming while the light is right. This is on union productions only. Your best chance of making a good income as an extra is to be a union member The best place to work is the Hollywood/Los Angeles area.

Yes, it is worth it if you are willing to pursue the jobs and the union membership. You also can do the extra work for the pleasure, especially if you do not live near major studio activity. The work can be enjoyable and you are likely to meet some people whose talent you have admired.

I was a hustler when it came to getting the available jobs for extras. I invested in my career by buying more wardrobe every month. I visited casting often enough to be known and not too often to be a pest.

Some of my friends who were extras became stunt performers. Many worked in high paying commercials. Some specialized in print work, aka modeling. Several worked as actors while they did extra work. I think each of them would agree it was all worth it.

CHAPTER 5: YOUR RESUME

When you begin your career your resume will look like Naked City. That is OK. I recommend a resume with your name in bold letters at the top. Next two lines, smaller font, your contact information with agency name, if you are represented by an agent. Also your height and weight and color of eyes and hair. That might seem unimportant, but it is critical for stand in work.

Next on the resume is your acting info beginning with Feature Films, next TV, next Commercials, then Stage and that could also include live music shows. Next, Acting Workshops and Other. That could include radio or internet or emcee work at the local lodge or bar or open mic experience. If there is no open mic show near where you live, start one. Start a theater group. Start a dance class or karate class. Get something going for your resume. I belonged to a drama workshop in Las Vegas that really helped me to become an extra.

For Feature Films and TV do not be afraid to write "None yet." Understand what a resume is. It is something for a casting director or interviewer to hold in their hands so they can ask questions. It is not a job ticket. Do not write in your resume that you played the part of Hamlet on stage if you did not. The interviewer might ask "Where did you appear in that play?" "Which city?" "What is your favorite line from that show?"
It is good to have your picture near the upper right of your resume, but that is not necessary. You will have your resume stapled to your head shot.

You should also carry some business cards with contact information and a small picture of your face. You might meet someone at a party or car wash or at a location site, while you are driving in the neighborhood. For extra work give your contact info to any A. D. but do not bother the director or actors on a set. You will gradually become a familiar face. .

Tom Willett

****
Height 6'4" SAG/AFTRA AFM MUSICIANS UNION   Weight 210#
Eyes Brown   Contact Agency 555-555-5555   Hair Brown & Grey

FEATURE FILMS

BUG BUSTER	Piano Player	DMG Entertainment
AIRPLANE 2	Dipstick Patient	Paramount
MELVIN & HOWARD	Kissing Cowboy	Universal

TV

HAPPY DAYS	Abe Lincoln	Paramount
MORK & MINDY	Abe Lincoln	Paramount
DEAR JOHN	Tom (Cast Member)	Paramount

COMMERCIALS
List on request

LIVE SHOWS

Singer, Guitar and Piano Player		Palomino Club
Stand up Comedy	Make Believe Ballroom	ABC TV
Stand up Comedy		Comedy Store

SPECIAL SKILLS AND ABILITIES AND TRAINING
Singing, fifties style, guitar and rockabilly piano, courtroom artist, pool and billiards, Abe Lincoln character, ex military, weightlifter Trained at Joe Behar's Community Drama Workshop.

****

Above is a sample resume template. I have changed contact info. Your resume can be formatted in a similar way but with your own information, of course. This is the actor's resume which you will want to have available if you need it. For extra work you can give this type of resume to an extra casting agency, but you will probably not need it on any set where you are working as an extra. Many extras do go on auditions for speaking parts on their days off, so it is good to have a resume.

When you are working on any movie extra job you will have a place that is your room or holding area. It is good to bring a few resumes to the set just in case an opportunity arises. Do not hand out resumes to the production team or the director or actors.

I have been on sets where I exchanged resumes with some other extras. Some of them gave me some information about agents who were looking for actors to represent. I had several different agents who sent me on auditions for high paying acting jobs. Some were agents I met through tips from extras with whom I worked.

Some of the extras became very good friends of mine. There were a few extras who needed pictures. I was glad to take their head shot or their action pictures for their composite. I did that for free. The peer group you create can help you.

The resume is a conversation starter for extras on a set. Ask someone what they think of your resume and pictures and they will probably have some good suggestions.

If you have an agency that represents you for speaking parts in movies or TV, or an agent who sends you out for commercial auditions, they will probably want their logo on your resume.

Some resumes are on very fancy parchment paper. Some are on colored paper. Some look like they were made of silk. I always used plain white paper with plain black text for my resume. Each person is different. The resume should be styled like you.

It is safe to send a picture and resume to any casting call, but be careful. Do not sign any long term contract with anyone when you are starting out. Do not agree to give an agent any percent of your earnings, except for the actual jobs he gets for you. Never pay an agent more than or less than ten percent.

My best jobs in Hollywood I got without an agent or manager. A manager takes a big chunk of your pay. I cannot imagine myself ever having a manager. I did have some good agents. Be careful, especially if you are somewhere other than Hollywood.

Do not overload your resume with dozens of feature film and TV and commercial jobs, even if they are for real. Producers are very often looking for NEW faces. Be stable and as relaxed as possible while the casting director is chatting with you at an audition. Have a story ready about yourself. Often when a casting director is looking at your resume he or she will say, "Tell me something about yourself." Chat about that funny experience you had on the farm or on the freeway or about your first car or favorite food.

CHAPTER 6: YOUR PICTURES

The picture the extra casting agency has of you is most likely one that they took of you when you registered. Find out when they have visiting hours. Take your own pictures in, even if they do not accept them. Let them see you in a tux in a photo, or a cowboy outfit. If you are a lady get some pictures of yourself with different hair styles and formal gowns and business attire or anything you see frequently in movies and TV.

Find out what size pictures they will accept. Have great pictures, but not necessarily professional pictures. The pictures that got me the most work were the "selfies" I took with a delayed timer lens.

For head shots, both eyes should show and the picture should give the viewer an idea what you are thinking. Take a picture of you looking at a tasty pizza and imagine how great it will taste. That is what the casting person will think is your "love look." For a gangster or gangsta look, wear a light colored tie with a dark colored shirt and, if you have one, a pin stripe suit with wide lapels. One of the clothing articles for men and women that creates a "character look" is a hat. Have many hats. Bow ties for men and scarves for ladies. For some, swim suit pictures are recommended.

For three quarter and full length body shots, have sporting attire or use a prop that has no logo. No Coke bottle. The audition or interview might be for Pepsi. No logo on any of your clothes, including baseball caps and tee shirts.

If you have period clothing, have some photos in those clothes. Old vests and shawls and hats. Good props include pool cues, tools like saws or hammers for men. Playing cards for men and women. A coffee cup, not hiding the face or a bouquet for the ladies. No puppies or kitties.

This picture was taken inside my Hollywood apartment. It was a "selfie" as most of my pictures were. It got me movie work for scenes where I would "finger synch" to music that had been recorded before..

It is good for a guy to have the mandatory face and shoulders, sport coat and tie, looking toward the camera and smiling shot, but think of who you are and what you can do and have some pictures that will get you some work.

Update your pictures with casting, especially if you change your hair style or color. Even if they do not accept the pictures, take them in on visiting days and you will burn the image into their minds. If you ride a unicycle or juggle, show them the pictures. You are the salesman or saleswoman and you are the product you are selling.

CHAPTER 7: A FEW OF MY EXPERIENCES

I have kept a reasonably good diary of my days in the entertainment business before the camera. I have worked more than 800 jobs. Most of the jobs were one day, but some were two or five and one job was seventeen days. When I worked as a cast member of the TV series Dear John, each episode was five days, except for holiday weeks when we worked four days. The 800 jobs does not count any of my radio shows or live stage shows or stand up comedy or open mic performances.

The 800 plus jobs began in 1957 and continued until 2005. There was a 22 year gap after my 1957 TV appearance on Make Believe Ballroom and my next appearance on camera in a movie called Players, starring Dean Paul Martin. I did not have a car in Los Angeles in the 1950s and I also did not know how the movie extra system worked. I spent my time wisely, working in a warehouse and becoming very stable. I also began to learn how to play the piano. Those things helped me get into the business.

I moved from California to New York City in 1960. Nothing show business related happened for me there. I moved to Las Vegas in 1961 and things began to happen. I worked at the EG&G warehouse. One of the employees at the EG&G warehouse had a night time radio show at KENO Radio. He became a friend of mine. I soon found myself writing comedy for his show. He used my one liners and jokes about the music and recording business on his show.

In February of 1962 he became too ill to talk. He had laryngitis. He asked me to do his show that night. It was February 26th. I gladly agreed. We went to the radio station and I looked at all the equipment. Bill would turn the dials and I would talk. The Midnight news items came across the UPI teletype. I read the news which included a mention of Liz Taylor's 30th birthday on February 27th, which had just begun. I introduced each song and pressed the play buttons for the turntables. I said some funny things. I was able to do radio. Bill was sick for two more nights and I filled in those nights. By the third night I was pressing all the buttons and turning all the knobs and taking meter readings. I was a deejay.

Radio would be my ticket to show business success. I balanced my steady job at the warehouse with weekend radio part time work. I was hired by KVEG Radio in 1963 to be one of their regular weekend announcers. I did a remote broadcast for KVEG from Sproul Homes in Charleston Heights, which was part of Las Vegas. One of their sales persons was Gil Frye,. He had once been a busy Hollywood extra. I learned a lot from him.

During the 1960s I worked at many Las Vegas radio stations on a part time basis. I worked a forty hour weekly job at the EG&G warehouse. EG&G was a big corporation in Las Vegas which did government contract work at the Nevada Test Site. It was a very good job and I made enough money that I did not need the pay from the radio stations. I was continuing to practice songs on the piano and I owned an early electric piano made by Wurlitzer. It had an earphone jack so I could practice as loudly as I wanted without disturbing my neighbors.

I owned my own record company and publishing company. In 1963 I began to produce my own records. The stations where I worked played some of my records but not all of them.

In the 1970s I began to work full time in radio and I also stated playing piano and singing at a piano bar. Small time show business success, but something big was about to happen for me. One of the deejays at a station where I worked was an actor who appeared in movies occasionally. I heard him mention where he would be working in the movie Electric Horseman. I went there to the filming location and I saw the lady who worked with Nevada Motion Picture services. I had met her once before at my drama workshop which I attended each week. She provided movie extras for many of the companies that filmed in Las Vegas.

I had registered with her a few months earlier and she remembered me. I told her I was available. She arranged for me to work Electric Horseman as part of a crowd scene the following week.

The lady was Jaki Baskow. I had met her at Joe Behar's Community Drama Workshop. That was a group of mostly young entertainers who were trying to make it in show business as actors and comics and musicians and performers of all types. I was not planning to go to the workshop that night, but fate intervened.

My young friend, Rocco, came to my home one night. He also had show business aspirations. He mentioned he wanted to be a dancer. I had never known that and I asked him to dance. He was great. He moved like Gene Kelly or Fred Astaire. I told him about the workshop.

I asked him to come to the workshop and meet everyone and he would be welcomed as a talented dancer who would have marvelous opportunities in Las Vegas shows. He agreed to come, but he did not show up. I did show up, however, and I met Jaki Baskow. She got me into the movie Players but there was no pay for my first job as a spectator at a tennis match.

I did meet Jaki, and when my radio friend did his scene on Electric Horseman, I was there to meet her again. She started giving me about one job every month with Union pay. She arranged to get me into the Screen Extras Guild, which cost, maybe $150 initiation at that time. That was one of the greatest bargains of my life.

Meeting Jaki the second time was important for me. In the world of entertainment it is good to be seen by casting people often enough they will remember you. Go to events where casting people are likely to be.

I worked in six movies in Las Vegas in 1979 and 1980. Some of the movies were pretty good. One was not very good, in my opinion. The movie Players, about tennis was quite boring to watch, but it was a real movie and I was in it.

The good movies were, Electric Horseman, Melvin and Howard, Going in Style, Smokey and the Bandit 2 and Pleasure Palace. My best scene was in Melvin and Howard where I was a cowboy bridegroom kissing Mary Steenburgen. In the other movies I worked with Art Carney, George Burns, Omar Sharif, Burt Reynolds, Jackie Gleason and Willie Nelson.

I also worked six episodes of VEGA$, the TV series. I stood in for Robert Urich one day when his regular stand in had to take the day off. When Robert came on the set he saw me standing in for him. He said, "Hey, you got the big guy standing in for me."

I also worked an episode of B.J. And the Bear. That was the only time I worked with Slim Pickins, He was just like you would expect. Very relaxed. Greg Evigan was nice and I would work with him later in Los Angeles.

I also worked on a Natural Lite Beer commercial. That turned out to be a big money day because they did three commercials in one day. I think it was a ten second and a fifteen second and a thirty second spot. At that time it was my biggest money day ever.

I did a lot in Las Vegas. It was easier for me to get into the world of background actor work by starting in Las Vegas, instead of trying to start in Hollywood. I was well established in Las Vegas. I was a known quantity. I was a deejay and I was a musician and a singer and I had met a lot of people who were in the movie business because of my radio work.

Remember, your personality counts. It is very important to shake hands with people and belong to a drama workshop or peer group of entertainers. Meet people, not just once, but a second time. Do not be just a singer or just a dancer. Be an entertainer who is seen as influential.

I moved to Hollywood in April of 1980. I was already in the Screen Extras Guild. I transferred from Las Vegas to Hollywood. I registered with about five extra casting agencies, including Central Casting. Yes, there is a Central Casting.

I started to work almost immediately. Then I suddenly stopped working almost immediately. There was a strike by Screen Actors Guild against the movie and TV productions. The strike lasted for three months. I got some part time work as a salesman and I waited out the strike. I would have preferred to have worked at a piano bar or in radio, but I did not find work there in the Los Angeles area in entertainment. My savings were beginning to run out.

The strike began on July 21, 1980, while I was working on Quincy, ME, a TV series. I was called back to Quincy on October 14, 1980. I was back on the set and I had made it through the strike. I was a working Hollywood extra. I was in the movies in Hollywood.

I started working a lot. I averaged about three days per week on the sets, and between working days I was on the phone waiting for one of the casting agencies to answer. In the 1980s I relied on my phone, my answering machine, my calling service and my beeper to help me get work.

Every month I would invest in some wardrobe items that I could use for movies and TV. Soon I had 1940s, 1950s, 1960s and current 1980s suits and ties and shirts and shoes. My closet will filling up fast.

If the movie scene was a formal dance, I wore my tux. If it was a Western street scene, I had the cowboy clothes, including a vest with lapels. Then came sweaters for those shows that had Winter scenes on hot days.

A costume shop was going out of business in Hollywood. I invested in their wig sale. I could become a blonde or redhead or older gray haired guy with just a change of hairpiece. The Lincoln beard was a big help for my career. Not only could I be in a scene as Honest Abe, but I had a new reason to take a picture of myself in a new outfit and use it as an excuse to visit casting. I was taking selfies long before the word was invented.

Pictures of my car helped me get work. I had a 1969 Rambler station wagon. My car was just right for some suburban neighborhood sets where a camera was filming a street scene. In the 1980s the car check was an extra $27 over the regular background day's pay.

I made a lot of money between 1980 and 1988 and then my luck got even better. I was recognized by many Assistant Directors who would sometimes request me on their shows. I worked several hundred jobs as a Hollywood movie extra. Then in April of 1988 I overheard a conversation between two guys on a set. The conversation led to my big break in Hollywood. I was now just two or three steps away from being a TV star.

CHAPTER 8: DEAR JOHN

I was working at Fox studios on some show as a background actor in 1988. There was a break and I had time to use the phone on the stage to call in for work the following day. Someone was on the phone and a couple of other guys were taking a break in the area. I was standing near a couple of guys who were talking and I overheard their conversation. One of the fellows was telling the other he had an audition the following day at Paramount. He mentioned the time and said it would be "...on the Amen stage."

Amen was a popular sitcom that filmed at Paramount. I made a mental note of what he had said, with the intention of going on the audition if I did not get a job for tomorrow. All I knew from the conversation was the audition was for an upscale New York City guy who was going to a meeting of divorced people.

One of the rules in Hollywood is you do not "crash" an audition. You are supposed to go to only those auditions to which you have been invited. That never stopped me. I invited myself. When I heard "New York City, divorced, upscale..." I knew the character immediately and I felt sure the other guys on the interview would all guess the character wrong.

I occasionally got a feeling when I went on auditions that I was able to understand the character better than anyone else in the room. Each time I had that feeling I was picked for the part. There also were times when I would go on an audition and I would see another actor who had figured out the character better than I had. I would say to myself, "He's got it."

The Amen stage was a sea of about 40 people auditioning for the part. I looked around at the guys in their 1980s suits and ties, all looking very nice and up to date.. They got the "upscale" right.

What they did not get right was "divorced." I gave the character a reason to be divorced. I wore a 1950s, immaculate suit with a wide tie and wide lapels and pleated pants. My character was upscale and 30 years behind the times.

Ed. Weinberger and James Burrows came onto the stage. Ed. was the Executive Producer and James would be directing. Ed. spelled his name with a period. Ed. saw me and turned to James and said, "That's him." The audition was over. I had the job.

Dear John started as a pilot, which meant there was a budget for one episode. That show would air and the producers would try to sell it as an ongoing series to a network. Most pilots are not sold. They show one time and then they become fond memories for the writers and actors, and not so fond memories for the producers and investors.

Dear John became a series on NBC in 1988. It received good ratings and it lasted until 1992. After it left NBC it became a syndicated show. It has been running somewhere ever since. It is not available on DVD at this time.

I was an actor in the show and I received residual checks when the show ran in syndication. If anyone tells you you cannot make it as an extra, they do not know what they are talking about. John Wayne was a movie extra. James Dean was a movie extra. Dennis O'Keefe was a movie extra. The list of stars who once were extras includes; Brad Pitt, Sylvester Stallone, Clint Eastwood, Renee Zelweger, Marilyn Monroe, Matt Damon, Bruce Willis. Jackie Chan, Channing Tatum and me and maybe you.

In addition to the financial rewards of being a cast member in a prime time sitcom, there were other fun perks. I had a parking space inside Paramount Studios. I had my own dressing room. I received fan mail. I did interviews with various newspapers and magazines. I received a lot of Dear John promo items, such as the Dear John jacket and robe and other printed collectibles. One Christmas I received a Paramount blanket which I still use to this day. I met and chatted with many movie stars who were guests on the show.

My point in mentioning this is to show you how much difference one day, one interview, one decision after hearing a conversation, can make in your career. I often invited myself to auditions. Sometimes it did not work out well for me. It worked out well for me in 1988 when I auditioned for Dear John without an invitation. It happened for me more than once, but once was enough. Know the rules and know when to bend or break the rules.

CHAPTER 9: TRAINING

Wherever you live, if there is a local theater group or drama workshop, join it. If there is no local acting or entertainment or drama workshop, start one. You can be the director of a weekly group meeting to gain experience on a stage or in front of a group in a living room.

Practice comedy routines with an audience of your peers. Perform music with a guitar or keyboard or do a dramatic scene. Learn how to act and react. Learn microphone technique and makeup tricks. Use a video camera to record your scenes for a future demo reel. Make YouTube videos.

This might sound like something that will not be helpful. It will be a great boost as you begin your career. You will meet other like minded entertainers who will exchange ideas and information with you about upcoming movie productions they might have heard mentioned somewhere.

The workshop I attended in Las Vegas for about four years was very instrumental in getting me into movies. A guest speaker who mentioned she needed some extras for upcoming films and TV shows turned out to be a legitimate talent provider for professional productions.

There are other kinds of training you can focus on. Learn to play an instrument. It is not that hard. Learn to play piano chords and guitar chords. Both of those skills got me work. Learn to drive a stick shift car. Learn to juggle. Can you flip a pancake in the kitchen? That might get you a commercial. Learn to play any sport. Do not just sit by the phone waiting for someone to call you to be in their movie. Have some skills listed on your resume. Dance. Deal cards like a Las Vegas blackjack player.

Whatever job you have, if it involves a special skill, list that on your resume. If you drive a fork lift, let that be known. If you are a good artist you might be needed as a courtroom artist. If you are a bowler, good or bad, that could definitely get you a job in a movie bowling scene. Can you swim well? Have that on your resume.

If you are not good at many things right now, train for some things. Learn from YouTube tutorials how to do some things you have always wanted to do. Learn close order drill for military scenes. Learn what the "corner man" does in a fight scene. Learn how to balance a tray of food as you walk through a restaurant for a waiter scene.

Do you know a little about first aid? Can you take someone's blood pressure reading? Most paramedics and nurses in hospital scenes are extras. Learn those skills and list them on your resume. Have pictures of yourself in white or green hospital smocks. Also candy striper outfits would be good for your portfolio of pictures.

I have worked with extras on unicycles, ventriloquist extras with their dummies, bathing suit guys and gals, floral arrangers and bakers. Learn the skills that you see in the movie scenes. Learn the basics of placing the bets in a casino scene for the closeup hand insert of picking up the chips and rolling the dice. You know it is going to be in many movies so learn it and list it as one of your skills.

To practice some acting parts that you will be doing if you work a lot of extra jobs, try drinking a cup of coffee. Actually try drinking from an empty cup and still look like you are sipping coffee. Never eat the prop food, unless they tell you to do so, but look like you are eating and drinking and talking with no actual sound coming out of your mouth. Almost every movie has a diner or restaurant scene. One of my extra friends in Hollywood specialized in being a waiter in movies and TV shows. He actually had worked in a restaurant and he knew the correct way to place the plates on the table and take them away. That is a skill to list.

One of my movie extra friends was a diver. He was trying out for the Olympics. He worked many swimming scenes because the casting people thought of him as a high board diver and therefor he was a swimmer and therefor he was called for beach scenes.

When I worked on Something Wicked This Way Comes, there was an extra who knew how to make the cotton candy for the carnival scene. You probably can learn that from YouTube videos. Train for anything you can imagine yourself actually doing in a movie or TV show.

I was never a good dancer, but I had a book that showed the basic steps for most ballroom dances. I danced in many movies and TV shows because I trained to be able to do the basics.

I did not ride horses, although many of my friends did. It paid more than being on the sidewalk in a Western movie. My thought about that was I could do better on the ground by staying where the action was taking place in .a saloon or in front of the Sheriff's office or walking across the street .

I worked out in gyms a lot when I was younger. I was strong and able to lift some heavy weights, but I was never put in a gym scene. I first used a computer in the 1970s, but I was never in a computer scene in the 1980s when I was so busy as an extra. I could walk on my hands, but they never used me for that. I could do pushups, but they never used me for that. I had worked in recording studios and radio stations but I was never in a movie scene with microphones or tape recorders. My point is, they might not use every one of your skills and abilities, but they will use some.

Be ready with some words also, just in case you are upgraded to a speaking part. Be ready to say, "May I take your order?" Be ready to say, "Dearly beloved, we are gathered here to join these two in the bonds of holy matrimony..." Be ready to say "Freeze. You are under arrest. You have the right to remain silent." Be prepared in case they want you to say, "Yes sir, Captain."

Be realistic about who you are and train for the parts you are most likely to be chosen to perform. Practice in front of a mirror to have a deadpan expression or a nice smile or a look of shock or grief. Practice taking off your glasses and wiping them with a tissue. Practice flipping a coin or putting on your lipstick without a mirror or opening and closing a door silently. You will probably be doing all these kinds of things.

If you take some karate lessons, that could be helpful in some action movies. Just having the outfit for karate classes or gym attire can be a door opener. Have pictures to show those skills you have and those you are learning.

Can you operate special equipment such as welding torches and tire changing tools? Let that be known to your extra casting agent. Learn how to use a bow and arrow or how to tie a bow tie. Learn anything that you want to do in a movie sometime.

Your best training will be the experiences you have in a drama workshop where you will be given an opportunity each week to perform skits and scenes. You will receive instant feedback from the other members of the group and you will be able to see your performance on camera, if you are using camcorders to assist in the workshop. Maybe you are good with expressions and you can see how to improve even more. You will see something in a movie or TV show and say "I want to learn how to do that." Learn it, get a picture of yourself doing it and you have another reason to visit casting.

Train yourself to remain calm in the middle of a movie set. Stage fright is very normal, but do not worry about it. Just proceed with your acting part, background or foreground, and you will find that the nervous feeling becomes a positive energy. You will do very well. Do not use any artificial means to gain composure. You will be at your best when you are yourself. Never stop learning.

TOM WILLETT

This 1980s "selfie" got me a lot of work. The priest's shirt and collar cost about $20. Each time I used it in a movie or TV show I was paid an additional $15 wardrobe allowance.

Remember, the producer does not want me or you in the movie or TV show. The producer wants my skills and abilities and my wardrobe and my training and my car. That same producer wants your wardrobe and your special abilities and your training and your car. Think like that and you will stay busy. When they call you by your first name, they want YOU. Some extras are invited to the wrap parties because they fit in with the production team spirit.. Pay close attention to everything that happens on a set when you are working.

CHAPTER 10: MY MOVIES & TV SHOWS

When I was 17 I arrived in Hollywood. I wanted to get into movies and TV and I wanted to make records and be on the radio. I did all that, but not at age 17. I did manage to get on the Make Believe Ballroom TV variety show with Al Jarvis when I was 18. That actually was pretty good for someone who had no experience. I auditioned as a comic and Al liked what I did and he put me on the show. I learned many years later that in Hollywood the working actor gets about one gig for every thirty auditions.

After being in front of a camera in a major production in 1957, it would be twenty-two years before I worked in that capacity again. I moved to New York City in 1960 and stayed there until I moved to Las Vegas in 1961. I did not do anything related to show business in New York City

In Las Vegas I did not appear in front of a camera right away. I worked my regular daytime job at EG&G and I started working radio on weekends. I also made a few records. I owned my own record company and I started a publishing company for my songwriting efforts. I began to do a few live music and comedy shows. Then in 1979 I appeared in a movie as a paid extra for the first time.

The first movie for me was Players. It was a tennis movie. I was in some crowd scenes. Soon after that I worked in my first episode of VEGA$. I would appear in six episodes of that show before I moved to California. I also worked in Electric Horseman and Pleasure Palace, a TV movie, and a Lite Beer commercial. After Players all my extra work was union pay scale.

My best job in Las Vegas when I worked as an extra, was in Melvin and Howard. I kissed Mary Steenburgen in a wedding chapel scene. I was dressed as a cowboy. I wore the same cowboy outfit in a scene outside the Alladin Hotel in a movie called Going in Style.

Las Vegas is also where I worked on BJ and the Bear and Smokey and the Bandit 2. I knew this was what I wanted to do. I belonged to AFTRA, which is the American Federation of Television and Radio Artists and I belonged to the Musician's Union and I had just been invited to join the Screen Extras Guild, which I quickly joined. Then I moved to Los Angeles.

In 1980 I began to work in movies and TV in Los Angeles, better known as Hollywood. I lived in a nice apartment that was in Hollywood, within walking distance of the Chinese Theater. I also could walk to Capitol Records and the Pantages Theater, where Academy Awards once were given to famous actors and directors.

I had what I needed. I had a phone. I had a car. I was registered with several casting agencies. I had a map of Los Angeles, so I could find my way to each location. I was stable. I had a good attitude.

On one of my earliest California jobs one of the extras told me he did not work very often. He told me, speaking about the extra casting agents, "They just hire their favorites."

I said, "That makes it easy. I will just become a favorite." That is what I did. The fellow I was talking with saw it as a problem that someone hired their favorite people. It made perfect sense to me.

I began to accumulate every type of wardrobe I could find that I could use in movies or TV shows. It was a slow process. I started with one suit. Within five years I would have more than 30 suits. Some from the 1950s and other decades. Hollywood tends to make movies from different eras. To work on them you need to look right.

I had cowboy boots and hats and a police uniform which cost about $200 counting the leather gear. My Abe Lincoln outfit got me a couple of extra days at high pay each year. That does not sound like much, but add that to a few cowboy days each year and a few days as a priest and a few days as someone in a tuxedo, etc.

I tried to work one day and call in for work the next. I could get by well on three days work each week and three months each year of something called "hiatus," when there was very little work to be had.

If you live somewhere other than sunny California, there might be many days each year when there will be nothing working.

My total number of days worked I have never figured out. I worked a lot between 1980 and 1992. I worked mainly as an extra. From 1988 until 1992, I was an actor and member of the cast of Dear John. I worked The People's Choice Awards as a singer and spokesperson and dancer late in 1988. I worked as a stand in and a photo double and an extra and an actor and a piano player. I worked as an extra in movies and TV and in commercials.

I had become a favorite of the casting people at each of the agencies where I was registered. I had gained some credibility in the Hollywood world of entertainment.

Now for some numbers. These are my numbers and I will mention some numbers of other people about whom I am familiar. I worked more than 800 jobs between 1979 and 2006 when I left California. That is 800 different jobs, not days worked. Most jobs were one day. Some jobs were two days. One job was seventeen days when I stood in on Under The Rainbow. Each episode of Dear John was an average of five days. Holiday shows were four days in length.

The numbers I am giving here are only for the jobs or gigs I worked in front of a camera in a feature film or TV movie or TV episodic show of some kind. This does not count my days and nights in radio or my live music shows or my YouTube videos or recording studio work.

I worked a lot. I was one of the top ten percent of busy extras in the Hollywood area, especially in the 1980s. I worked more than 100 feature films and more than 140 TV shows. I worked Quincy, ME and Hill Street Blues more than fifteen times each. I worked as a regular in The Misadventures of Sheriff Lobo. I was a regular on some short lived shows, such as Eye to Eye and Strike Force.

My numbers were pretty good, but I did have a friend, Arthur Tovey, who worked more than one thousand movies. He worked from 1923 until 1993. Arthur stood in on Gone With The Wind, He worked with Clark Gable, Elvis Presley, Orson Welles, Audie Murphy, Cecil B. DeMille, Rita Hayworth and George Clooney. He had stories about each of the famous people with whom he worked in Hollywood. He had been to Oliver Hardy's house on several occasions for visits.

Another interesting number is sixteen. If you are in a union movie as an extra and are a union member you will get a day's pay for each hour that goes past sixteen hours. Fourteen hour days are common in movies. Stand ins are in the best position to be in a Golden Hour situation. That;s what they call it.

I worked with some fun people in my twenty-five plus years in the business. Some of the names include; Jonathan Winters, Burt Reynolds, Judd Hirsch, Clint Eastwood, Jackie Gleason, Mickey Rooney, Arnold Schwarzenegger, Madonna, Pee Wee Herman, Richard Simmons, Robin Williams, Lana Turner, Elizabeth Taylor, Mel Ferrer, Jane Wyman, Andy Griffith, Mel Brooks, Charleton Heston, Harrison Ford, Bubba Smith, Warren Beatty, Debbie Allen, Anthony Newley and Luciano Pavarotti just to name a few.

I had nice conversations with Rock Hudson and Will Sampson and Lana Turner and each of the cast members and guests who appeared in the show Dear John. Warren Beatty talked with me several times while we worked on a scene in Reds. Jim Carrey came over to where I was standing to talk with me about the snacks on the movie Man on the Moon. The only reason I mention these people is to let you know what to expect.

I also was in the company of great directors, such as John Huston, who complimented my singing on the set of Annie. He would listen to our trio of entertainers as we performed between takes on the movie. I worked with Richard Brooks on the set of Wrong is Right with Sean Connery on the day President Reagan was shot. I worked with Sydney Pollack and Jonathan Demme and Brian De Palma.

I worked with famous actors who directed their own movies. Clint Eastwood, Warren Beatty, Carl Reiner, Sylvester Stallone and Mel Brooks Many TV actors also directed their shows. I worked with Larry Hagman on Dallas when he was directing and acting in the scenes. Michael Landon directed and starred in Little House on the Prairie and Highway to Heaven . Leonard Nemoy directed some of the TV episodes on which I worked as an extra. Ray Danton was once a famous actor who became a TV director. I worked with him when he directed an episode of Quincy, ME.

Some of the shows I worked had numbers in the title. Smokey and the Bandit 2, Sting 2. Psycho 2. Airplane 2: the Sequel. Two of a Kind. I actually worked two projects that had the working title "Two of a Kind." One was a TV movie with Robbie Benson and George Burns. The other was a feature with John Travolta and Olivia Newton John. That working title was later changed to Second Chance.

Speaking of movie extra work I have done, I will tell a few stories about standing in for different actors. If you decide to pursue stand in work, it is rewarding and also very demanding of your total attention. If you are a good communicator and you can chat with big name stars without gushing, stand in work and photo doubling might be something you will want to try when you start working as an extra.

I have stood in for Harvey Korman, Mel Ferrer, Kenneth Mars, Pat McCormick, John Lithgow, Bob Urich, Chevy Chase, Christopher Lee, James Cromwell and others. I was a utility stand in on some shows which meant I would stand in for several actors each day during the set up for their scenes.

I was a photo double for Chevy Chase, James Cromwell, Michael Conrad and Pat McCormick. That meant they photographed my back during some over the shoulder shots when the actor was getting ready for a different scene.

If you decide to try standing in, you will find there is a relationship between the actor and the stand in. You will tell the actor, when he or she gets ready to step into place for the scene, any changes that were made after the rehearsal. You might say, "John, they changed your walk from going left of the chair to right of the chair. Your new mark is here."

You should be good with small talk to keep the set calm. You also will likely "run lines" with your actor. You will read the other actor's lines to help your actor rehearse.

The relationship between actor and stand in can vary from set to set. Some actors might decide to let the assistant director choose his stand in. Other actors have their stand in chosen and they give instructions to the A.D. About who stands in for them.

I worked with Rock Hudson for the first time in a TV movie called The Star Maker in 1981. He was a very friendly person and an excellent actor. In one scene we did I noticed that Rock and I were the same height and we had nearly identical builds. During a break I mentioned to the A.D. That if he needed a stand in for Rock at any time in the future, I was experienced.

The assistant director told me he had no say in naming a stand in for Rock Hudson because Rock specified his stand in by name in his contract. That is loyalty. It was still a good thing I mentioned standing in, however, because the A.D. did ask me to do some utility standing in later in the day for a tall actor in one scene. In 1981 that meant an extra $10.

When I worked as a stand in for Mel Ferrer on Falcon Crest, an interesting situation occurred. We filmed at Notre Dame High School, which is in Sherman Oaks. Mel was a nice, very quiet, somewhat shy person who was very much at home wearing a tuxedo and dancing in a palace. Mel was starring in the episode and directing the show. On the set at the Burbank Studios he was comfortable giving the directions to the actors and crew.

I was from a farm boy, warehouse working, truck driver background and I was a bit rough around the edges compared to Mel, but we had a good working relationship. Everything went well at the studio.

We had the camera set up in one hallway at the school. Classes were still in session. Students were not supposed to be in this particular area on the day of filming. The assistant directors were away doing some work away from camera. The only people near the camera were Mel and myself and a couple of members of the camera crew.

A few young male students suddenly appeared in the hallway in front of the camera. They wore what Central Casting might have called "gang attire." They were talking loudly and laughing and making some remarks about the TV production company working there in their school. I glanced around and noticed their was no AD nearby. Mel looked very uncomfortable and almost like he feared some problem would happen.

Most sets have a police officer, not on official duty, but retired or off work but in uniform, who handles all crowd control. The policeman was not there. The A.D. Was not there. Mel was not comfortable with the situation.

I walked over to the teen age boys and said, "Hi, Guys. Can I get you to stand over here behind the camera? We will be shooting in this direction and you will be able to see all that happens. If you have any questions about what is happening, just ask me."

The students listened to what I said and moved behind camera and kept very quiet except for a few questions. They were very nice and well behaved and caused no problems.

The thing that I remember most about that day was after the students were in a good place behind camera, before the A.D. and the cast were back to do the scene, Mel Ferrer came over to me. He bent his head down a bit and whispered to me "Thank you."

If you do decide to stand in, become more than a statue. Be someone who helps your actor with your special abilities or your courtesy or whatever works to aid your relationship.

I have known stand ins who pitched a softball back and forth with their actor. Other stand ins took messages for their actor on the stage phone when the actor was in rehearsal.

On the short lived TV sitcom Nutt House, I stood in for Harvey Korman. Harvey had worked for many years with Tim Conway. Tim would call the set and ask for Harvey. If Harvey was busy rehearsing, I would take his calls. Tim would say something like "You tell that no good bum Harvey Korman he will never make it in Hollywood. Tell him Mr. Conway said he's getting tired of carrying your dead weight."

I would go to the set and say, "Mr. Korman, there is a Mr. Conway on the phone. He said to tell you that you have no talent and that he is tired of carrying your dead weight."

Then Harvey would giggle a bit and regain his composure and say something like, "You tell Mr. Conway that Mr. Korman said Mr. Conway couldn't act his way out of a paper bag. Also tell him my toilet is stopped up and I need him to bring a plunger." It really was that much fun. A stand in is a combination of silent actor and friend and helper with whatever comes along.

During my years in Hollywood I received only two movie credits. One was for standing in on Under the Rainbow. The other was for being a band member in Bug Buster. Both times my last name was misspelled.

Hollywood really is a place where a person can go from rags to riches almost overnight. For me the turnaround started when I overheard a conversation about an upcoming audition. The next step was going on the audition and being picked for a job, After that was a waiting period of several months for the pilot to be sold. Then the show started and I was along for the four year ride.

I made more money during the first four years of Dear John than I had made in the previous 50 plus years of my life. I would make even more when the show became syndicated for the next four years. It could happen to you. There is a lot of money in Hollywood and it changes hands every day. You do not have to chase the money. Stay busy and the money will find you.

Some of the movies in which I appeared where I am seen doing my extra background acting include, Naked Gun (watching Leslie Nielsen shooting at a runaway police car), Airplane 2 (having my oil checked as a hospital patient and holding a revolver to my head in the same hospital sequence), Deal of the Century (I am an Air Force colonel in a desk scene early in the movie), Melvin and Howard (kissing cowboy), Uncommon Valor (military officer in back of crowd at 1 hour thirty nine minutes and thirty seconds into movie), Pee Wee's Big Adventure, (trucker in restaurant up close about forty three minutes, thirty-eight seconds into movie), I Desire aka Desire, the Vampire (policeman) and Kiss, Kiss, Bang, Bang (Abe Lincoln late in movie). There are many dozens of other movies in which I worked but those are the more visible appearances for me.

I worked with stars from the Golden Age of movies, such as Kirk Douglas, Burt Lancaster, Liz Taylor, Rock Hudson, Van Johnson, Mickey Rooney, Charleton Heston, Roddy McDowall, Sylvia Sidney and John Houseman to name a few.

I have worked with action and adventure stars such as Sylvester Stallone, Harrison Ford, Arnold Schwarzenegger,, Pierce Brosnan and Burt Reynolds.

I worked with some sports stars like Magic Johnson, Andre the Giant, John Matusak, Lyle Alzado and Lou Ferigno.

I have worked with so many wonderful and talented people that I could write a book.

With Pam Dawber and Robin Williams at Paramount on the set of Mork and Mindy. Robin has a smaller hat size than Abe.

CHAPTER 11: REVIEW

If you have decided to become a movie and TV extra and you live in one of the United States, that is a goal you can make a reality. Every state has some movie or TV or commercial production. Usually the major productions are in the big cities. If you live on a farm or in the mountains, you can still become an extra, but it will require you to be more aggressive.

You are not too old or too young. You are not too tall or short. Whatever you see as your shortcoming the director might see as a requirement. Be positive. Have pictures to show even if the casting director does not accept the pictures right away.

If you live in Hollywood you could become a person who works background action several days each week. If you live in Las Vegas or San Francisco, you could work several days each month. If you live in a major Midwestern city, you could work several days each year. If you live in a small town that is somewhat isolated, you could work a few days or more each year if you plan your route to success.

If I were just starting in the business now, I would be sure to have a flexible job oi I would work from home, so I could accept work when it suddenly became available. When you get a day's work as an extra you will get about twelve to sixteen hours notice. You will get the phone call maybe at four PM and your call time the next day is six or eight AM. Sometimes earlier. You must be ready and have transportation,

If I were starting in a city somewhere away from Hollywood, I would invest in a vintage car. I would maybe get a Cadillac or Lincoln limousine and a chauffeur's cap. I would have a priest's outfit. Women would be wise to have a formal gown or two and men should have a tux. I would take martial arts training. I would attend a drama workshop or start one. I would have a resume that listed my special skills and abilities. I would learn some dance steps. In small towns or remote locations it is a good idea to increase your value to each production.

Chances are you can take better pictures of yourself for movie roles than a professional photographer. Your picture should show both eyes and what you are thinking.

The Assistant Director is the person who gives the extras instructions on the set. It might be the Second Assistant Director or the Trainee Assistant Director. The casting agency gives the job to the extra. You register with a casting agency that casts movie background performers and usually they will tell you when to call for work, or they will call you. They might charge you approximately $25 to take your picture and put it in the file. Do not let that stop you from bringing in more pictures in different wardrobe. Remember, they cannot unsee you as whatever you are in your picture. If you are a cowboy in a photo and a business person in the picture they have on file, they will still think of you as a cowboy if the need for a Western character comes along and they have seen your picture as a cowboy

You know they need you. Be nice and low key but give them information about some special training you had. When I realized the movies did not want me, they wanted my wardrobe and car and special abilities, I found myself in demand.

Become a stand in if you can. Read IMDB information to get the height of various actors and actresses. If someone is coming to your area to do a movie and they are your height, ask the A.D. or casting director if you can be their stand in. The stand in works every day the actor works. If you become a stand in just discuss the scene with your actor. Do not gush about the actor's past movie roles. If you do talk about things other than the scene, usually the weather or traffic are safe places to venture. The actor has lines to remember. Have a calm conversation.

If you are serious about becoming a busy extra who makes a living wage, read all the information at SAG/AFTRA.org that pertains to you. Click on Member Services and click Membership from the drop down menu. Then click the link for How To Join SAG/AFTRA. Brace yourself for the initiation fee and the requirements to join. Then do it. Join.

There are SAG/AFTRA locals in Arizona-Utah, Atlanta, Chicago, Colorado, Dallas Fort-Worth, Hawaii, Houston-Austin, Los Angeles, Miami, Missouri Valley, Michigan, Nashville, Nevada, New England, New Mexico, New Orleans, New York, Ohio-Pittsburg, Philadelphia, Portland, San Diego, San Francisco-Northern California, Seattle, Twin Cities and Washington-Mid Atlantic.

I started my extra career in Nevada. It was easier for me to get in being a big fish in a small pond. Once I was in the Screen Extras Guild I moved to Hollywood where Hollywood productions were now in play for me.

Remember also to check with local agencies in your area and Film Commissions. A film commission is in most major cities and in every state. They might have a different name, such as Governor's Commission of the Arts. They would be especially helpful if you have a vintage car or two or a windmill on your property or something special a producer might want to use in his or her film.

This is a picture I took of myself when I bought my police uniform. I gave copies to every extra casting agency with which I was registered. I worked many days in this uniform on shows such as The Misadventures of Sheriff Lobo, T. J. Hooker and I, Desire, aka Desire, the Vampire.

If you decide to make a living as a movie extra, or just try to get into one production, you will have some good stories to tell for years to come. Movie making is exciting at times and you never know what will come next. I would not change any of the crazy things I have done for a thirty year office job.

ABOUT THE AUTHOR

Tom Willett started his movie extra career in Las Vegas in the late 1970s. In 1980 he moved to Hollywood and started working as a background actor in movies, TV shows and commercials. He worked in more than 800 total productions in front of the camera. He was a stand in, a photo double, an actor and a musician in shows filmed or taped in Southern California and Las Vegas, Nevada. That does not count his many live music shows or radio work or recording studio sessions.

Tom's career began when he learned some information about a need for extras in movies in Las Vegas. He heard the info in a drama workshop he attended. Tom acted quickly when he found out about incoming movie productions. He worked about once a month in movies in Las Vegas and he decided it would be better to move to Hollywood. He moved there in 1980. Tom became one of Hollywood's busiest extras in the 1980s.

Tom is now retired and spends his time making YouTube videos for his Featureman channel. Tom learned how it is possible to be upwardly mobile as an extra by having the right wardrobe and the right attitude.

Tom has a page at IMDB where his name is Tom Willett (I). It lists many of the shows he worked and has a bit of a bio.

The cover photo shows Tom as an Elk Man in the TV movie Fugitive From the Empire, The Archer Strikes Back. It is also known as The Archer.

Made in the USA
Columbia, SC
22 November 2020

25206168R00024